Eyes on the Sky

Black Holes

by Don Nardo

KIDHAVEN
PRESS™

THOMSON
———✦———
GALE

San Diego • Detroit • New York • San Francisco • Cleveland
New Haven, Conn. • Waterville, Maine • London • Munich

Cover Photo and Title Page photo: © Julian Baum/Photo Researchers
© AFP/CORBIS, 27
Associated Press, AP, 30
© Julian Baum/Photo Researchers, 5, 25
© Julian Baum/Science Source/Photo Researchers, 22
© Jean-Loup Charmet/Science Source/Photo Researchers, 9
© Lynette Cook/Science Source/Photo Researchers, 17
© CORBIS, 31
© J. Foster/Photo Researchers, 11
© Mark Garlick/Science Source/Photo Researchers, 19
© Victor Habbick Visions/Science Source/Photo Researchers, 39, 42
© David A. Hardy/Science Source/Photo Researchers, 36, 37
© Roger Harris/Science Source/Photo Researchers, 34
© Laguna Design/Science Source/Photo Researchers, 21
© Jon Lomberg/Science Source/Photo Researchers, 13
© Max-Planck-Institut Fur Extraterrestrische, Physik/Science Source/Photo Researchers, 28
Brandy Noon, 15, 18, 41
© Bill Sanderson/Photo Researchers, 7

For more information, contact
KidHaven Press
27500 Drake Rd.
Farmington Hills, MI 48331-3535
Or you can visit our Internet site at http://www.gale.com

LIBRARY OF CONGRESS CATALOGING-IN-PUBLICATION DATA

Nardo, Don, 1947–
  Black holes / by Don Nardo.
    p. cm.—(Eyes on the sky)
  Includes bibliographical references.
  Contents: Predicting black holes — How black holes form — Detecting black
holes — Black holes as cosmic gateways?
    ISBN 0-7377-1366-6 (hardback : acid-free paper)
  1. Black holes (Astronomy)—Juvenile literature. [1. Black holes (Astronomy)]
  I. Title. II. Series.
    QB843 .B55 N37   2003
    523.8'875—dc21

2001004104

Printed in the United States of America

Table of Contents

1

Predicting Black Holes

Black holes are among the most mysterious and fascinating objects known to exist. Unfortunately, their name is partly misleading. This is because they are not really holes in space, as sometimes pictured in popular fiction. A hole is an empty void. By contrast, black holes are objects with substantial **mass**, or a measurable quantity of matter. So they are actually quite the opposite of holes.

Simply put, a black hole is an object made up of a very large amount of matter packed into an extremely **dense**, or compact, state. All matter has **gravity**, a force or property that attracts other matter. Earth's gravity attracts the moon, for example, and holds it in orbit around the planet. But the gravity of a black hole

Astronomers believe that this galaxy, which they call M87, has a giant black hole in its center.

dwarfs that of planets and moons. A black hole's gravity is so great that even light cannot escape it. And that is why it appears black.

Indeed, the concepts of gravity and black holes are intimately linked. One cannot talk about one without discussing the other; and black holes are a logical result of gravity operating under extreme conditions. That is why scientists predicted the existence of these bizarre objects long before they found any evidence for them.

Newton and Gravity

The first major theory of gravity was proposed by English scientist Isaac Newton in the late 1600s. He used mathematics to show how various objects with mass attract one another. In fact, he said, the force of gravity exerted by an object is directly related to the amount of its mass. A small object has very little mass. So it exerts very little gravitational pull. By contrast, a large object, such as a planet, has a great amount of mass. So its gravity is capable of attracting cars, people, mountains, and moons.

The force of gravity is also related to distance, Newton showed. The farther apart two objects are, the less their gravities attract each other. Conversely, the closer two objects are, the stronger they attract each other. Thus, Earth easily maintains its hold on the moon, which is

Englishman Isaac Newton was the first scientist to explain how gravity works.

relatively near. But Earth's gravity has no measurable effect on the planet Mars, which is much farther away.

Of course, if Earth had enough mass, it *could* attract Mars. That is why the sun is able to hold Mars in orbit. The sun is considerably farther away from Mars than Earth is; but the sun is also much more massive than Earth.

Escape Velocity and "Dark Bodies"

According to Newton's theory, Mars and Earth cannot escape the sun's gravity at their present speeds. But if these planets could suddenly move faster, they might escape. The speed that a body needs to move to escape the gravity of another body is called its **escape velocity**. The escape velocity of Earth is about seven miles per second. So rockets launched from Earth, for example, must attain that speed to break free of its gravity.

Not surprisingly, the more massive an object is, the higher its escape velocity. In 1783 English scientist John Michell carried this idea to its natural extreme. In theory, he said, stars with tremendous mass might exist. The gravity of such a star would be huge, as would its escape velocity.

Michell wondered what would happen if the star's escape velocity exceeded the speed of light—186,000 miles per second. In that case, he reasoned, even light could not escape the star. So it would not be visible to human eyes. Appropriately, Michell called these objects "invisible

French scientist Pierre-Simon LaPlace suggested the existence of "dark bodies," now known as black holes.

stars." In 1795 French scientist Pierre-Simon LaPlace also theorized about such supermassive objects. He called them "dark bodies."

In Michell's and LaPlace's time, no evidence yet existed for invisible stars and dark bodies; so these precursors of black holes were little more than a scientific curiosity. For a long time afterward few researchers discussed them.

Einstein and Curved Space

However, in the early twentieth century scientific interest in the concept of black holes revived. This was the result of a new theory of gravity proposed by German scientist Albert Einstein. His ideas greatly altered the way humans view space and the objects within it. These ideas also allowed scientists to understand and predict black holes more confidently.

Einstein explained the workings of gravity differently than Newton had. Newton had described gravity as a force exerted by objects. In contrast, Einstein argued that gravity is a property of space itself. Before Einstein, scientists assumed that space was an empty void; they thought this void had no ability to affect the objects that move within it. But Einstein said that space has invisible properties, among them a "fabric" with an elastic, or bendable, quality.

Objects with mass that are moving through space interact with this hidden fabric, Einstein stated. Such an object sinks into the fabric, creating a depression in it. Moreover, the more massive the object is, the deeper the depression. Thus, very massive objects distort or curve the fabric of space; this curve is what people experience as gravity.

An artist's view of gases spiraling into the gravity well of a black hole.

Consider two planets of differing size approaching each other. The smaller planet runs into the curve of the larger object's depression, or "**gravity well**." Soon, the smaller planet rolls "downhill" toward the larger one. This is like the larger planet "pulling in" the smaller one in Newtonian terms. If the smaller planet is moving fast enough, it can roll back out of the other's gravity well and escape. If not, it remains trapped. And it either orbits or crashes into the larger planet.

Bending and Trapping Light

Einstein and other scientists wanted to test and prove this theory. If gravity wells exist, they reasoned, a very deep one should affect a beam of light. Light travels fast enough to allow the beam to escape the well; but the well should bend the beam enough for scientists to measure it.

The sun seemed the logical choice for the test. It is the largest object in our solar system, so in theory, its gravity well would be the deepest. The experiment occurred during an eclipse of the sun in 1919. The moon temporarily blocked the sun's image. And stars could be seen near the sun's edge. Scientists found that beams of light from these stars did indeed bend slightly as they passed by the sun; moreover, the beams bent by nearly the exact amount predicted by Einstein.

The experiment's success confirmed Einstein's theory of **curved space**. It also opened up an exciting new field of inquiry. It had been shown that the sun's gravity well bends light a little bit; so it stood to reason that a much more massive object would bend light even more. This raised the question of a supermassive, superdense object. Could such an object actually

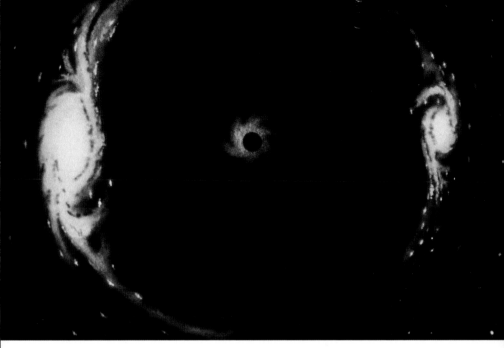

A black hole's immense gravity bends light from the surrounding stars.

trap light within its extremely deep gravity well? In the 1930s scientists predicted such superdense objects. And in 1967 a scholar at Princeton University, John Wheeler, coined a term to describe them—black holes.

Prediction was only the first step in understanding and studying black holes. Two important questions remained. First, how do they form? Second, how could humans find them? Fortunately, the answers to these questions were not long in coming.

2

How Black Holes Form

In the early twentieth century, scientists established that in theory black holes might exist. But if so, how could such superdense objects form? Logically, to compress huge amounts of matter into a very small space would require extreme violence. Numerous violent events occur in nature. On Earth, these include hurricanes, earthquakes, and volcanic eruptions; while on a planetary scale, asteroids and moons crash into planets with devastating results. Yet none of these disasters is nearly violent enough to compress matter into a superdense object.

To explain black holes, therefore, scientists turned to violence on a stellar scale. (The term stellar refers to stars.) Just as humans are born,

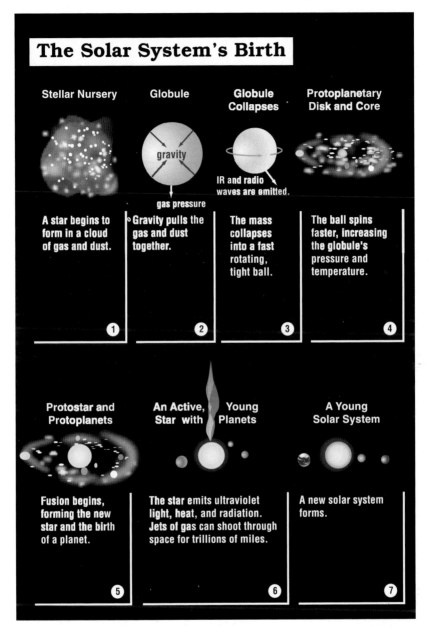

The Solar System's Birth

Stellar Nursery

A star begins to form in a cloud of gas and dust.

①

Globule

gravity

gas pressure

Gravity pulls the gas and dust together.

②

Globule Collapses

IR and radio waves are emitted.

The mass collapses into a fast rotating, tight ball.

③

Protoplanetary Disk and Core

The ball spins faster, increasing the globule's pressure and temperature.

④

Protostar and Protoplanets

Fusion begins, forming the new star and the birth of a planet.

⑤

An Active, Young Star with Planets

The star emits ultraviolet light, heat, and radiation. Jets of gas can shoot through space for trillions of miles.

⑥

A Young Solar System

A new solar system forms.

⑦

live out their lives, and finally die, stars, including our sun, also undergo a life cycle. A star emerges out of a large cloud of gas and dust. Gravity causes the cloud to contract over time;

and this causes the gases to heat up. Eventually the temperature at the core of the cloud grows hot enough to ignite nuclear reactions. And in a great burst of light, the star is born.

For billions of years the star shines, giving off light and warmth. But finally it uses up all of its fuel and enters its death throes. A terrible catastrophe occurs in which most of the star's matter becomes very dense. Scientists call this disaster "**stellar collapse**." Depending on the star's initial size, various superdense objects can form. And one of these is a black hole.

Opposing Forces Inside a Star

No danger exists of a star collapsing and creating a superdense object as long as that star remains stable. A star typically remains stable for billions of years. This is possible because two immense forces within the star oppose and balance each other. The first of these forces is gravity. Gravity causes the huge amount of matter in the star's outer layers to press inward with enormous power.

The second force at work in a star is the outward flow of energy from the core. The nuclear reactions occurring there release gigantic amounts of heat, light, and tiny particles. Take the example of the sun. Each and every second, the sun's core creates energy equivalent to that released by 100 million nuclear bombs. The

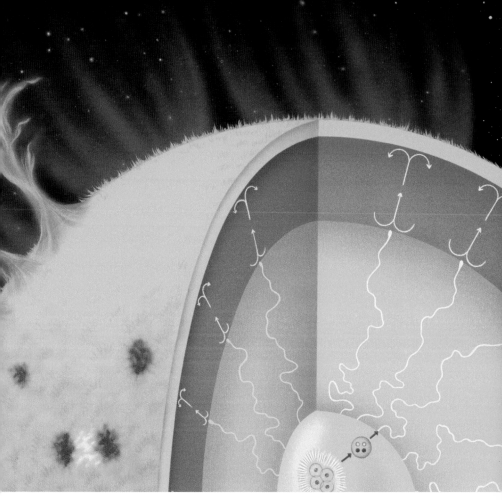

This drawing shows huge amounts of energy pushing outward from the sun's core.

huge stream of energy travels outward from the core; and the force of this moving energy exerts a great amount of outward pressure.

Fortunately for humanity, these great forces in the sun pose no danger to the star or Earth. The force of energy pushing outward balances the force of gravity pushing inward. So the sun maintains its structure and remains stable.

The Sun's Death

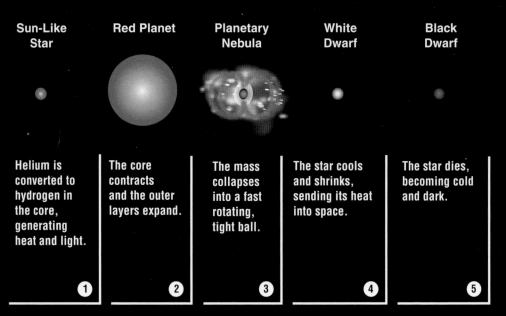

Sun-Like Star	Red Planet	Planetary Nebula	White Dwarf	Black Dwarf
Helium is converted to hydrogen in the core, generating heat and light.	The core contracts and the outer layers expand.	The mass collapses into a fast rotating, tight ball.	The star cools and shrinks, sending its heat into space.	The star dies, becoming cold and dark.
1	**2**	**3**	**4**	**5**

Scientists estimate that the sun will continue in this stable state for several more billion years.

White Dwarfs and Neutron Stars

Eventually, however, the sun, like all stars, will run out of the elements that fuel the nuclear reactions in its core. When that happens, the delicate balance that keeps the star stable will be upset. The outward pressure of escaping energy will diminish. This will allow it to be overcome by the inward pressure of gravity.

With the forces inside the sun now out of balance, disaster will be inevitable. Some of the star's outer material will escape into space. But most will collapse inward with extreme violence. The forces involved will be so great they will crush most of the matter into a small ball about the size of Earth. Astronomers call such an object a **white dwarf**. A white dwarf is so dense that a tablespoon of its material weighs a thousand tons. Not surprisingly, such an object has a very deep gravity well. To escape it, an object would have to attain a velocity of about three thousand miles per second!

To become a white dwarf is the ultimate fate of an average-sized star like the sun. But some stars are larger than the sun. They have more mass and stronger gravities; so their collapse is more violent and creates an object even more dense than a white dwarf. Scientists call such an object a **neutron star**. A tablespoon of

Captured in this photo is a neutron star, a super-dense object with enormous gravity.

neutron star material weighs at least several trillion tons. And its escape velocity is nearly 125,000 miles per second, about two-thirds the speed of light.

A Bottomless Pit

Clearly, light is just barely able to escape the deep gravity well of a neutron star. It stands to reason, then, that an even denser object would actually trap light inside its well. And that is exactly what happens in a black hole.

A black hole forms from the collapse of a star many times the mass of the sun. The force of the collapse is so large that it does not stop at the white dwarf or neutron star stages. Instead, the rush of matter down the star's gravity well continues on and on. Atoms are ripped apart and their remnants packed tightly together.

The final result is an object so dense and massive that its escape velocity is greater than the speed of light. Indeed, the gravity well of a black hole is like a bottomless pit. Nothing that enters it, including light, can escape it. Another way of visualizing it is to imagine the collapsing matter falling down the object's gravity well. The well seems to get deeper and narrower forever; so the matter seems to keep falling forever.

Because a black hole is so dense, it packs a very large amount of material into a very small volume of space. So such an object is often sur-

Computer animation depicts the steep gravity well of a black hole.

prisingly small. For example, if our Earth was suddenly converted into black hole material, it would be about the size of golf ball.

Of course, Earth is not a star. So it cannot become a black hole. How big are black holes that form from stellar collapse? No one knows for sure. But scientists estimate that one created by the death of a star eight times the sun's mass would be about the size of a small house. Most of the former star's matter would still be inside the black hole. So the tiny object's gravity would be about the same as the star's. Suppose that the star had planets orbiting it when it collapsed. Most of these would continue to orbit the black hole. They would not be sucked into the black hole unless they strayed too close to it.

Are Black Holes Dangerous?

Still, any life that might have existed on such planets would be wiped out. Most living things would die from powerful radiation released during the star's collapse; and any survivors

A large black hole sucks in gases and dust, which spiral into it.

would freeze to death after the star ceased giving off light and heat.

Usually these lethal effects would remain localized. Because the distances between stars are very great, most black holes that form this way would pose little or no threat to neighboring stars and their planets. Only in regions where many large stars lie very close together would the danger increase. Then a black hole might suck in stars and planets and over time grow much larger. In a sense it would become a monster with a huge appetite. Incredibly, recent evidence shows that such cosmic monsters do exist.

3

Detecting
Black Holes

A fter predicting black holes and describing how they might form, scientists naturally wanted to know if they actually exist. But detecting these strange objects presents a unique challenge. Light cannot escape a black hole; so it appears black and invisible to human eyes and telescopes. Because the existence of black holes cannot be confirmed by direct means, scientists must resort to indirect means. Namely, they try to observe the way these mysterious objects affect matter around them.

An Invisible Companion?

First, theory predicts that a black hole has tremendous mass. Therefore, its strong gravity should attract or affect the movements of nearby objects. Take the example of a binary star. A binary star is a system of two stars that move through space together. They orbit each other, bound by their mutual gravities; and the gravity of one affects the movements of the other in predictable, measurable ways. Binary stars are common and astronomers have studied many of them.

What if one star in a binary system collapsed and became a black hole? In theory, the black hole and its companion star would continue to orbit each other as before. And the companion star would still move like a member of a binary pair. Yet when scientists scanned the area around the star, they would see nothing. This could lead them to only one conclusion. The star must have an invisible partner.

The black hole of a binary star system pulls gases off its companion star.

Moreover, if the partner's mass was large, it would likely be a black hole.

The Point of No Return

Another possible way of finding black holes is by detecting radiation created near them. In the twentieth century, scientists began detecting X rays from outer space. X rays are a highly energetic form of radiation. Evidence showed that every star gives off some X rays along with visible light and other types of radiation.

In theory, scientists should be able to use X rays to locate a black hole. Of course, the rays could not come from the object itself; after all, not even light and other kinds of radiation can escape its gravity well. However, as a black hole moves through space, it encounters gas, dust, and other debris. As the debris draws close to the object, it spirals into its gravity well.

On the way into the black hole, the debris passes what might be termed "the point of no return." Scientists call this the **event horizon**. As long as matter remains outside the event horizon, it has a chance of escaping. But once it crosses the event horizon, it is forever lost in the bottomless pit of the black hole. The distance from the center of a black hole to the event horizon is called the Schwarzschild radius. It is named for German astronomer Karl Schwarzschild, who first described it. This dis-

X rays are released near the event horizon of this huge black hole.

tance varies, depending on the black hole's mass. The Schwarzschild radius of a black hole having ten times the sun's mass is estimated to be about twenty miles.

Now consider what happens to space debris that approaches the event horizon. It spirals ever closer, getting hotter and hotter. Finally, the black hole's immense gravity tears apart the atoms in the debris. And in the process they give off a strong burst of X rays. An instant later, the smashed up matter disappears forever beyond the event horizon. But the X rays it emitted continue to travel outward; when they finally reach Earth, they reveal the position of the black hole.

Cygnus X-1 and X-Ray Binaries

To find a black hole, therefore, scientists needed to locate a strong X-ray source where no star existed. Or they needed to find a binary star system with an invisible partner. As luck would have it, they found a situation that met both these conditions.

This photo shows Cygnus X-1, a binary star system thought to contain a black hole.

In 1962 instruments on Earth detected a strong X-ray source. It is located in the constellation of Cygnus; so it became known as Cygnus X-1. When astronomers observed Cygnus X-1, they saw that it is an invisible partner in a binary system. Most became convinced that Cygnus X-1 is a black hole created by the collapse of a large star.

Since the discovery of Cygnus X-1, other **X-ray binaries** have been found. Each consists of two stars, one of which is very dense and gives off large quantities of X rays. Most often, the denser star lies fairly close to its companion. The denser star's gravity draws gases from the outer layers of the companion; and these gases spiral in toward the denser star, releasing X rays. Some of the X-ray sources in these systems are white dwarfs. Others are neutron stars. But when no star can be detected at the source of the X rays, scientists suspect the presence of a black hole.

Galactic Black Holes

The black holes that are believed to exist in binary-star systems typically have masses of about three to fifty times that of the sun. But evidence suggests that much bigger black holes exist. In recent years astronomers have devoted much attention to the cores of **galaxies**. A galaxy is a group of many billions of stars

This distant galaxy, which astronomers call NGC 7742, likely has a giant black hole in its core.

held together by their mutual gravities. The local galaxy, in which the sun and its family reside, is called the Milky Way. Experts believe that gigantic black holes lurk at the center of the Milky Way and most other galaxies.

Trying to detect and measure such galactic black holes is very difficult. This is partly because the cores of galaxies are extremely distant. Even the center of our own galaxy is very far away. The sun orbits the center of the Milky Way at a distance of about twenty-six thousand **light years**. (A light year is the distance that light travels in a year, or about 6 trillion miles.)

However, new and very large telescopes and other advanced instruments have revealed a great deal about the Milky Way's core. There, many huge stars lie very close together. Some of these stars are 120 times the size of the sun or larger. What is more, most are moving very rapidly around an extremely massive object in the center of the core. The object, called Sagittarius A-star, has about 2.6 million times the sun's mass. Most scientists believe it is a supermassive black hole.

No Limit to a Black Hole's Size?

Sagittarius A-star has already pulled in and consumed more than 2 million stars. And it will likely continue to grow. Indeed, evidence shows that the supermassive black holes in many other galaxies are much larger. Andromeda, the nearest major galaxy to our Milky Way, has an object 30 million times heavier than the

Scientists believe a super dense object in the Andromeda galaxy thirty million times heavier than the sun may be a black hole.

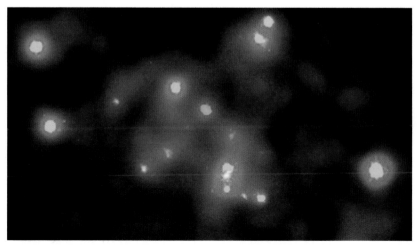

sun in its core. And in the center of a galaxy dubbed NGC 4261 lies an object with 1.2 billion times the sun's mass.

This suggests that there is no limit to how big a black hole can get. In fact, the ultimate fate of galaxies and the living things within them may be decided by these supermassive monsters. Consider the one lurking in the Milky Way's core. It is possible that several billion years from now, its gravity will draw our solar system, including Earth, into its black mouth.

4

Black Holes as Cosmic Gateways?

With the discovery of Cygnus X-1 in the 1960s, many people came to see black holes as more than mere theory. Suddenly, there seemed to be concrete evidence for their existence. Both scientists and nonscientists began to think seriously about the physical properties of black holes. On the one hand, they seemed to be a logical result of the extreme effects of gravity. On the other, they appeared to behave in bizarre ways, and their inner workings remained mysterious.

Not surprisingly, the mysterious aspects of black holes stimulated the human imagination. Some people tried to picture how they look beyond the event horizon. Would objects on the outside be visible from the inside? Also, a black hole seems to remove matter forever from the **universe**. Where does this lost matter go? Does it emerge somewhere else? And if so, might it be possible someday for people to go there, too?

Science fiction stories and films have come to exploit many of these mysterious aspects of black holes. Most often, they picture these superdense objects warping the fabric of space. That fabric becomes so distorted it tears. And this creates a small opening. The opening is a gateway leading into an invisible tunnel commonly referred to as a "**wormhole**."

In this artist's conception, the flash of light in the upper right corner is a wormhole opening in space.

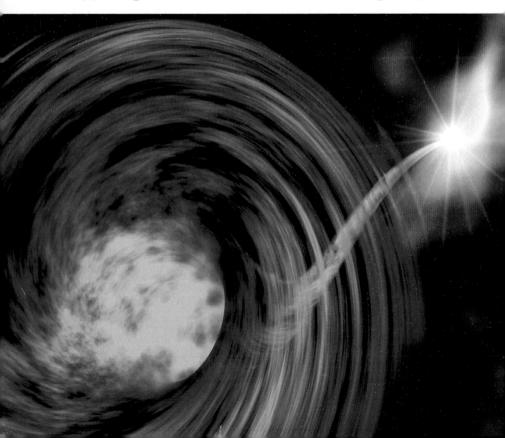

As portrayed in fiction, piloted spacecraft travel through these tunnels. In the *Star Trek* TV shows and movies, for example, humans and other intelligent beings often enter wormholes. They soon emerge in distant star systems or faraway regions of the galaxy; or they use the wormholes to travel backward or forward in time.

White Holes and Rings of Fire

Many people are surprised to learn that the concept of such cosmic gateways actually has a scientific basis. The first important exploration of the idea of wormholes came in 1935. Albert Einstein and a colleague, Nathan Rosen, used mathematics to describe what might lay beyond a black hole's event horizon. They suggested a black hole might open up a sort of tunnel. And that tunnel might connect with another black hole somewhere else. At first, scientists called these tunnels "Einstein-Rosen bridges," after the men who described them. Later, they came to be called wormholes as well.

Einstein and Rosen merely pointed out the mathematical possibility of such tunnels. They did not mean to suggest that people could travel through them. After all, scientists recognized that a black hole would possess enormous gravity. It stood to reason that any matter that entered such an object would be crushed into

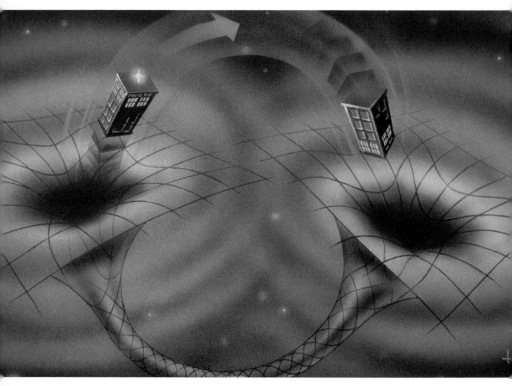

Wormholes allow objects to move freely through space and time in this imaginary view.

atoms. Even the atoms would be torn apart. So surely no object, living or nonliving, could survive intact. And even if it could, it would be trapped forever in the black hole's gravity well.

In the 1960s, however, new research revised this picture somewhat. Some scientists suggested that matter and light may not remain forever trapped inside a black hole. Instead, these substances might travel through a wormhole and emerge elsewhere. The exit point would be very bright; so it came to be called a "white hole."

New Zealand mathematician Roy Kerr also pointed out that black holes are probably not motionless. Instead, they are spinning, similar to the way Earth rotates on its axis. If so, said Kerr, the entrance to a black hole might be shaped like a ring. In a sense it would be a "ring of fire." Perhaps an object, even a spacecraft, could pass through the ring without being crushed. It might emerge in another part of the universe. Or it might end up in a completely different universe (assuming other universes exist).

Collapsing Wormholes and Exotic Matter

Some scientists rejected the idea of traveling unharmed through wormholes. They agreed

An artist shows a spacecraft exiting a wormhole near one of the moons of Jupiter (visible at upper left).

with the math that shows wormholes are possible. But they pointed out that such tunnels are likely to be very unstable. First, calculations suggested that a wormhole would open only for a brief instant; then, in a fraction of a second it would shrink and close. This would happen so fast that even light would not be able to enter the hole while it was open. How, then, could a spacecraft hope to get through?

The critics cited other problems as well. First, intense radiation near the entrance to a wormhole would probably fry the crew of an approaching spacecraft. Suppose, however, that the crew has managed to invent special shielding that protects them. They would still have to travel at impossible speeds; otherwise, they would not make it through the wormhole's entrance before it closes. And even if the craft *could* move fast enough to enter, its occupants would still be doomed. The tunnel would remain highly unstable. It could suddenly collapse, instantly crushing the craft and crew.

An Impossible Dream?

This makes traveling through wormholes look like an impossible dream. However, some scientists argue that the idea is not as hopeless as it seems. The main problem, they say, is finding a way to keep the wormhole stable and

This computer illustration shows a future space station exiting a wormhole.

open long enough for travelers to pass through. Keeping it open would require substantial pressure from the inside. Various kinds of matter—solids, liquids, and gases—exert pressure. But according to the math, ordinary matter is not strong enough to do the job.

What about *extraordinary* matter? Could some kind of stronger-than-normal matter exist? In the 1980s, scientists Michael Morris and Kip Thorne of the California Institute of Technology suggested that it might. They called it "exotic" matter. Many scientists think that exotic matter was common when the universe was very young. Perhaps small amounts of it still exist here and there in the universe. Or maybe an advanced race of beings has found a way to manufacture it. At present, no one can say; no direct evidence of exotic matter has yet been found.

Journeys Through Space and Time

If exotic matter does exist, or can be made, it might well keep wormholes stable. And that would allow the possibility of traveling through them. The question then arises: What benefit is there to such travel?

First, flying through wormholes might afford people shortcuts to faraway places. Consider the similar situation of a watermelon and an ant. The outer surface of the watermelon represents normal space, and the ant a space traveler. The ant wants to get to the opposite side of the watermelon. And walking at top speed, it will complete the trip in three minutes.

Shortly before leaving, however, the ant notices a nearby hole in the surface of the watermelon. Being adventurous, the creature enters the hole. It finds and follows a tunnel that leads through the center of the watermelon and emerges from another hole on the opposite

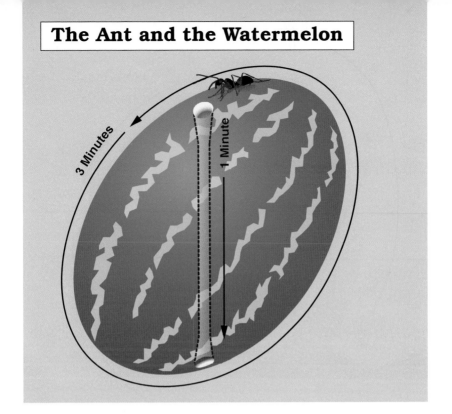

The Ant and the Watermelon

side. This route is more direct than the one on the surface. So the ant makes the trip in only a minute.

Similarly, humans in spacecraft might someday use wormholes to reach distant places more quickly. In so doing, they will also become time travelers of a sort. Einstein's calculations show that time slows down for fast-moving objects or people. And the faster one travels, the more time slows. To the crew of a spacecraft speeding through a wormhole, time will not *seem* to move slower; to them, all will appear normal. But during the trip more time will pass outside the wormhole than on the craft. The occupants may experience the passage of only a year as dozens

This imaginative drawing illustrates a wormhole as a gateway to other places and times.

or hundreds of years elapse in the outside world. So the crew will arrive at their destination in what they perceive as the future.

Wormholes and time travel are only two of many bizarre concepts associated with black holes. Others include collapsing stars, super-dense matter, bottomless gravity wells, and monsters devouring galaxies. As time goes on, more such oddities may well be discovered. Science has only just begun to unravel the mysteries of the strange and awesome objects called black holes.

Glossary

black hole: A superdense object with gravity so strong that not even light can escape it.

curved space: The concept, first advanced by German scientist Albert Einstein, that space has an invisible fabric that bends when objects with mass move through it.

dense: Highly compact.

escape velocity: The speed at which a body needs to move to escape the gravity of another body.

event horizon: The point of no return near a black hole. Any matter that crosses the event horizon disappears forever into the black hole.

galaxy: A gigantic group of stars held together by their mutual gravities. Our galaxy is called the Milky Way.

gravity: A force exerted by an object that attracts other objects. The pull of Earth's gravity keeps rocks, people, and houses from floating away into space. It also holds the moon in its orbit around Earth.

gravity well: A depression in the fabric of space created by the mass of an object. The more massive the object, the deeper the well.

light year: The distance that light travels in a year, about 6 trillion miles.

mass: The measurable matter making up an object.

neutron star: A superdense object that forms from the collapse of a large star.

stellar collapse: A violent event in which gravity causes a star to collapse inward on itself squashing most of its material into a small, very dense object.

universe: The sum total of all the space and matter known to exist.

white dwarf: A superdense object that forms from the collapse of an average-sized star.

wormhole: An invisible tunnel connecting a black hole to another spot in the universe.

X-ray binary: A double-star system in which one star collapses into a very dense object, usually a white dwarf, neutron star, or black hole.

For Further Exploration

Pam Beasant, *1000 Facts About Space.* New York: Kingfisher Books, 1992. An informative collection of basic facts about the stars, planets, asteroids, and other heavenly bodies.

Franklyn M. Branley, *Journey into a Black Hole.* New York: HarperCollins, 1986. One of the best children's books about black holes, it tells how a boy discusses these bizarre cosmic objects with a scientist and then imagines himself donning a spacesuit and entering a black hole. Both informative and humorous.

Heather Couper and Nigel Henbest, *Black Holes.* London: Dorling Kindersley, 1996. A handsomely illustrated book that explains the basic concepts surrounding black holes in easy terms for young people. Highly recommended.

Nigel Henbest, *DK Space Encyclopedia*. London: Dorling Kindersley, 1999. This beautifully mounted and critically acclaimed book is the best general source available for grade school readers about the wonders of space.

Robin Kerrod, *The Children's Space Atlas: A Voyage of Discovery for Young Astronauts*. Brookfield, CT: Millbrook Press, 1992. A well-written, informative explanation of the stars, planets, comets, asteroids, and other objects making up the universe.

Don Nardo, *Gravity*. San Diego: KidHaven Press, 2002. A thorough discussion of gravity and its effects, including explanations of white dwarfs, neutron stars, and black holes. Aimed at basic readers.

———, *The Solar System*. San Diego: KidHaven Press, 2003. This colorfully illustrated book describes the various members of the sun's family and ends by examining the probability that the solar system will eventually be absorbed by the giant black hole lurking in the center of our galaxy.

Index